Original title:
Quiet Halts Amid the Mermaid Huff

Copyright © 2025 Swan Charm

Author: Paulina Pähkel
ISBN HARDBACK: 978-1-80563-467-6
ISBN PAPERBACK: 978-1-80564-988-5

The Velvet Veil of Ocean's Breath

Beneath the waves where silence sighs,
A velvet veil in twilight lies,
Whispers of dreams in briny deep,
Call to the hearts that long to leap.

Stars above in a moonlit dance,
Guide the lost in a fleeting trance,
With every crest, the ocean's call,
Beckons the brave, enthralls them all.

In shimmering light of coral bright,
Secrets hidden from day and night,
Creatures roam in a watery waltz,
A symphony of nature's pulse.

Tides that rise and gently fall,
Echo the stories of one and all,
In currents strong, the past we trace,
Find solace in the ocean's grace.

So let the waves envelop you,
In their embrace, find something true,
For in the depth of the ocean's breath,
Lies the beauty of life and death.

Dappled Light on Slumbering Waters

Gentle rays through leaves descend,
Casting jewels where shadows blend.
Each ripple sings a soft refrain,
A tranquil heart, where dreams remain.

The cool embrace of twilight's breath,
Whispers tales of life and death.
In echoes sweet, the waters gleam,
A world awake, yet lost in dream.

Reflections of Serenity Undersea

Beneath the waves, where silence reigns,
A hidden world in soft refrains.
Colors dance, like fleeting sighs,
As time drifts by, the spirit flies.

Light filters down in gentle streams,
Where shadows weave through watery dreams.
Creatures glide in fleeting grace,
In this realm, we find our place.

Peacefulness in Deep Waters

Depths of blue, a quiet heart,
Where troubled thoughts are torn apart.
The subtle sway of liquid grace,
Welcomes the soul to find its space.

Soft whispers call from ocean's floor,
In currents deep, we seek for more.
A soothing balm, where worries cease,
In the ocean's arms, we find our peace.

An Ocean's Gentle Cradle

In the embrace of tidal signs,
The ocean rocks, where freedom shines.
A cradle made of foam and spray,
Where fleeting dreams are born each day.

Stars above in velvet skies,
Reflect the depths where magic lies.
In every wave, a story flows,
Of life and love, as knowledge grows.

The Reflective Depths of Slumber

In the quiet of night, shadows play,
Whispers of dreams drift softly away.
Crickets sing under the moon's soft glow,
As stars twinkle bright, in cosmic flow.

Waves of thought slip through gentle seams,
Carried by currents of woven dreams.
Memory's whispers, both distant and near,
In the blanket of night, they appear clear.

Veils of slumber, so sweetly spun,
Beneath the wings of the midnight sun.
Floating on clouds, on velvet so smooth,
Where fantasies dance and hopes gently soothe.

Seekers of truth in the silence abide,
Wandering paths where the echoing tide,
Reveals worlds hidden in soft, gentle light,
As shadows enchant, with their tender might.

Embrace the calm, where the heart finds peace,
In the depths of slumber, all troubles cease.
Awake with the dawn, with stories to tell,
Of reflective depths, where all dreams dwell.

Gentle Cradle of the Aquatic Realm

In a cradle of waves, where secrets lie,
Beneath the surface, where echoes sigh.
Coral gardens sway with a rhythmic grace,
In the aquatic realm's enchanting embrace.

Silver fish dart through the twilight sea,
Painting soft strokes of tranquility.
Bubbles rise softly, like whispers of dreams,
In the gentle currents, where magic beams.

The lull of the waters, a soothing song,
Guides weary travelers, where they belong.
Cradled in beauty of sapphire's gleam,
In the depths of the ocean, life finds its theme.

Mysterious shadows, in dance they merge,
In harmony's pulse, they silently surge.
Creatures of wonder in soft twilight roam,
In this gentle cradle, they find their home.

Raindrops create ripples, soft and light,
As day fades and welcomes the velvet night.
The aquatic realm, where hearts can be free,
Nurtures the spirit, like a tranquil sea.

Dreams in the Deep Abyss

In the deep abyss, where shadows dwell,
Whispers of secrets suspend like a spell.
Lost among echoes, time drifts away,
Carrying dreams in the depths' ballet.

Darkness enfolds like a velvety shroud,
Hiding beneath where the fish swirls proud.
Glimmers of bioluminescent glow,
Guide the lost souls in the ebb and flow.

Rippling patterns trace stories untold,
In the depths of the sea, both timid and bold.
Each tale a thread in the ocean's loom,
Woven together, dispelling the gloom.

The heartbeats of creatures crafted in night,
Dance to the rhythm of the moon's soft light.
In the abyss's cradle, we dream of the sky,
Where the surface world's glimmer seems to lie.

In silence, these visions unfold and partake,
Of the wonder that stirs when the sea starts to wake.
Capturing moments, the ocean's embrace,
Holds dreams in the depths, a sacred space.

Hidden Wonders in Silent Waters

In silent waters, where secrets are spun,
Hidden wonders bask in the soft, warm sun.
Under the surface, a world thrives unseen,
With life ever vibrant, so lush and serene.

Glistening scales flash in a dance full of grace,
As waves gently cradle this magical place.
Every ripple carries a story of old,
Of treasures and journeys, in whispers retold.

Lily pads float, like dreams on the breeze,
And dragonflies dart with the greatest of ease.
The silence cradles each tender sigh,
While nature composes its lullaby.

Beneath the blue, where the waters embrace,
Hidden wonders dwell, each finds its own space.
In tranquil reflections that shimmer and gleam,
The heart of the world holds its timeless dream.

So linger a while in this peaceful domain,
Where silent waters weave joy and refrain.
For in hidden wonders, both tender and small,
Lie the secrets of life that bind us all.

The Resting Place of Wandering Spirits

In the glade where shadows weave,
Whispers of the past believe.
Leaves that rustle, spirits call,
Echoes linger, hear them all.

Beneath the ancient willow's sway,
Lost souls wander, night and day.
Faintest light through branches streamed,
Guides the hearts that long have dreamed.

Moonlit paths of silver mist,
Phantoms dance, none can resist.
In their laughter, shadows twirl,
A world unseen begins to unfurl.

Where the nightingale sings low,
Dreamers find the map to go.
Through the mist, a flame does spark,
Leading home from journeys dark.

In the quiet of the eve,
Hope and longing intertwine, believe.
Wandering spirits find their place,
In the heart of time and space.

Ebb and Flow of Unseen Harmonies

Waves embrace the sandy shore,
Echoes of a distant lore.
Rhythms pulse beneath the foam,
Mysteries of the sea's vast dome.

In the hush where tides do blend,
Secrets whisper, messages send.
Shells that cradle ocean's sigh,
Carry tales where dreams may lie.

Moonlight drapes on tranquil seas,
Dancing light upon the breeze.
Nature weaves a symphony,
In each wave, a melody.

With each rise, with every fall,
Songs of life both great and small.
Harmony in every note,
In the heart, the sea's own boat.

Unseen threads of vibrant grace,
Binding all in time and space.
Ebb and flow, a timeless dance,
Invite the heart to take a chance.

The Pause of Light in Deep Waters

In the depths where silence reigns,
Light builds bridges, softly gains.
Ripples weave through darkened seas,
Whispers linger in the breeze.

Shadows hold their gentle sway,
In the stillness, peace does play.
Time stands still, a moment caught,
In the depths, all is sought.

Beneath the waves, reflections gleam,
Where the sun spills its golden dream.
Every flicker tells a tale,
Of journeys held and winds that sail.

Floating gently, thoughts arise,
In the pause, a world of skies.
Deep waters cradle thoughts of light,
Guiding dreams through endless night.

In this sanctuary's embrace,
Seek the depths, uncover grace.
Life's true essence, softly flows,
In deep waters, wisdom grows.

Submerged Dreams in the Silence of the Sea

Beneath the waves where silence lies,
Echoes of dreams in slumber rise.
Hidden treasures, lost in time,
Ballet of shadows, a rhythmic rhyme.

Coral gardens bloom and fade,
Whispers of hope in twilight made.
Each soft sigh of the tide's retreat,
Holds the secrets, bittersweet.

In the calm of a twilight haze,
Forgotten wishes softly blaze.
Every ripple, a love once known,
In the deep, we'll find our own.

Melodies trapped in ocean's heart,
Yearning souls, never apart.
Dancing softly with the tide,
In submerged dreams, we confide.

A lullaby in watery sleep,
Promises whispered, secrets keep.
In the silence, echoes stay,
Submerged dreams will find their way.

Beneath the Calm of Ocean Dreams

In shadows soft, the waters weave,
A tapestry where dreams believe,
The moonlit waves, they gently sigh,
As silver fish dance, flickering by.

With whispers sweet, the sea does call,
To sandy shores, where shadows fall,
Each grain, a story, lost in time,
A secret rhyme, a silent chime.

The currents sing of days gone past,
Where ancient tales forever last,
A siren's song beneath the swell,
In the deep blue, all is well.

Beneath the calm, the dreams take flight,
Through currents dark, to dawn's warm light,
With every crest and every trough,
The ocean whispers, soft and rough.

In twilight's grace, the stars align,
To guide the lost to shores divine,
Together in this liquid space,
We find our peace, our lasting grace.

Murmurs of the Forgotten Deep

In depths where silence wears a crown,
The echoes of lost worlds resound,
Forgotten ships with tales untold,
Lie resting deep in currents bold.

A gentle hum, the sea's lament,
Of ancient mariners, heaven-sent,
Their voices drift like misty dreams,
In hidden realms where starlight beams.

The ocean's breath is thick with sighs,
Each wave a secret, softly lies,
In coral gardens, life awaits,
To weave the threads of fates and mates.

The deep holds whispers of the past,
In currents deep, the lessons last,
With every pulse of rising tide,
The heart of ocean, vast and wide.

As night descends, the shadows play,
On shimmering paths where fish do sway,
Joining the dance of moonlit beams,
Unraveling our ocean dreams.

Lullabies of the Coral Abyss

In twilight's calm, the corals glow,
With vibrant hues, a gentle show,
Their whispered songs, a soothing balm,
In ocean's heart, a sacred calm.

The ebb and flow of tides embrace,
A lullaby in this soft space,
The anemones sway with grace,
In harmony, a sweet, soft place.

In shadows deep, the creatures glide,
Their secret lives, we must not hide,
Through tunnels tangled, life does creep,
As ocean weaves her songs so deep.

With every breath, the waters sigh,
A gentle hush, beneath the sky,
In rhythm's dance, the dolphins play,
Their laughter lights the dimming day.

So close your eyes and drift away,
In coral dreams, where peace will stay,
The sea shall sing you soft to sleep,
In lullabies, the ocean keeps.

Still Waters and Dreaming Tides

Upon the shore, the stillness lies,
With muted hues of twilight skies,
The water's glassy surface gleams,
Reflecting all our silent dreams.

A gentle breeze, a whisper soft,
Caresses waves that rise aloft,
As thoughts meander, float, and glide,
In tranquil depths where hopes abide.

Each ripple tells a tale of grace,
Of lives entwined in this vast space,
The ocean holds each fleeting thought,
In fleeting moments, love is sought.

The tides may change, but dreams remain,
In still waters, we feel no pain,
A union forged with every swell,
In tranquil moments, all is well.

So sit awhile, and let them guide,
On dreaming tides, our hearts confide,
In stillness found beneath the skies,
Where ocean whispers, never lies.

Solitary Moments at Dusk

As shadows stretch across the ground,
The whispers of the evening sound.
With twilight's brush, the sky ignites,
In solitude, I find my sights.

The fading light, a gentle sigh,
Flickers soft like fireflies.
Each breath a pause, the world concealed,
In this stillness, fate revealed.

A silver moon begins to rise,
Casting dreams through dusky skies.
I wander paths of muted grace,
In every step, a secret place.

The stars ignite within my heart,
Their brilliance forms a work of art.
Here in the quiet, I belong,
The dusk, my cloak, the dark, my song.

As night enfolds the day's embrace,
I find my peace in empty space.
With nature's pulse, I sit and bask,
In solitary moments, free to ask.

Tranquility in Aquatic Stillness

In the hush of water's flow,
Where gentle currents softly glow,
Reflections dance on glassy seas,
In aquatic calm, my spirit frees.

The rippling surface, pure and clear,
Echoes whispers drawing near.
Each droplet speaks of peace profound,
In tranquil depths, my heart is found.

Beneath the surface, life sways slow,
An underwater world in a quiet show.
I drift with thoughts like drifting leaves,
In stillness, magic quietly weaves.

Time dissolves where water meets sky,
And all my worries drift and die.
In this haven, I can remain,
Immersed in peace, untouched by pain.

With every breath, a new release,
In aquatic realms, I find my peace.
Lost in stillness, forever blessed,
In nature's arms, my soul finds rest.

The Serpent's Soft Lull

Beneath the boughs where shadows play,
A serpent glides, both sleek and gray.
With scales that shimmer in dappled light,
It weaves a tale of soft delight.

It curls upon the forest floor,
A silent whisper, ancient lore.
In gentle coils, it finds its ease,
Swaying slow with rustling leaves.

A lullaby of earth and air,
Enfolds the woods in soft despair.
Each hiss a song, each glide a dance,
In nature's realm, there's blissful trance.

The crickets chirp, the owls call,
While shadows deepen, nightfall's thrall.
In every flick and fleeting glance,
The serpent stirs the stillness' dance.

So let this moment linger long,
Where silence speaks the wild's deep song.
Embrace the dusk, the serpent's lull,
In its embrace, feel life is whole.

Muffled Songs of the Sea

Upon the shore where soft waves break,
A melody the ocean makes.
With each swell and gentle crash,
Muffled songs in a moonlit flash.

The stars above begin to sway,
As seafoam whispers night and day.
Each crest a tale, each trough a sigh,
In salty air, the echoes lie.

From depths unknown, the sirens call,
Their haunting tunes in shadows fall.
I close my eyes and drift away,
To where the tides and dreams display.

The sands absorb the ocean's heart,
As nature plays its timeless part.
In whispered tones, the sea conforms,
Embracing me within its arms.

So carry forth these notes of grace,
As waves explore the endless space.
In muffled songs, my spirit soars,
The ocean's love, forever yours.

The Sigh of Calm Currents

In twilight's glow, the waters gleam,
A gentle hush, a soothing dream.
The whispers soft, like secrets shared,
In the embrace of night, all is bared.

With every wave, the world stands still,
Nature's pulse, a tranquil thrill.
In silvered light, the shadows play,
While time rests easy, drifting away.

The moonlight dances upon the sea,
A serenade of serenity.
Hearts find calm in the ebb and flow,
In the quiet, their fears let go.

With stars above, like jewels bright,
The water twinkles, pure delight.
A soft embrace in life's embrace,
Here in stillness, we find our place.

Whispers of the Ocean's Heart

Beneath the waves, a tale unfolds,
Of ancient songs, and secrets bold.
The ocean's heart, a beating drum,
Calls to the souls, to all who come.

With every tide, a voice so clear,
As whispers float, we start to hear.
The echo of time, in currents deep,
A lullaby that lulls to sleep.

Seashells gather wisdom old,
Their stories wrapped in stories told.
The mystery of the sea's embrace,
Holds the dreams of every place.

In salty air, the echoes blend,
Every wave a message sends.
The ocean calls with gentle grace,
Inviting us to find our space.

The Beauty of Stilled Waters

A mirrored lake at break of dawn,
Reflects the golden hues of morn.
The beauty lies in quiet streams,
Where nature holds its whispered dreams.

The surface smooth as glassy glaze,
Unfolds the light in gentle ways.
The ripples dance with tender care,
Each moment cherished, ever rare.

Among the reeds, the stories bloom,
In whispers carried, nature's tune.
The beauty sings of tranquil grace,
In every corner, a warm embrace.

With every breath, the silence speaks,
In joyous laughter, the heart seeks.
The stillness here, a sacred art,
Leaves traces of peace within the heart.

Murmurs of an Undersea Haven

In depths below, where shadows play,
A haven stirs, in soft array.
The murmur of life, both bright and rare,
As coral blooms, a kingdom there.

Every fish a flash of color bright,
Gliding through the water's light.
In harmony, they weave and sway,
An undersea ballet on display.

The whispers of currents, soothing sound,
In this refuge, peace is found.
With every turn, surprises greet,
A world of wonder at our feet.

Among the kelp, the stories spin,
Of playful seals and journeys kin.
An underwater realm of grace,
In every corner, a soft embrace.

Soft Echoes of Neptune's Lament

In deep blue waters, whispers flow,
A tale of loss where shadows grow.
Neptune sighs beneath the waves,
His heart entwined with those he braves.

Lost sailors sing in the salty air,
With every crash, a burden they bear.
Echoes dance on the brine-kissed breeze,
Filling the night with mysterious pleas.

Moonlit tides reveal old scars,
As starlit dreams drift amongst the jars.
Shimmering hope in each cresting swell,
A sorrowful song, a secret to tell.

Calm Amidst the Ocean's Heart

Beneath the waves, a silence reigns,
Where time dissolves and peace remains.
Gentle currents cradle the night,
A tranquil world, devoid of fright.

Here shadows twirl in a graceful dance,
Amidst the calm, life takes a chance.
A lullaby sung by the tide's caress,
Whispers of love, a soft redress.

The ocean's heart beats deep and slow,
In every ebb, a tale to sow.
Serenity veils the vast domain,
Where dreams are born, and hope's not slain.

Secrets Cradled by the Sea Mist

Veils of mist, the ocean's gown,
Hiding treasures, lost and found.
Beneath the foam, stories await,
Tales of wonder, spun by fate.

Shells whisper softly, secrets their own,
Crafted by time, in silence grown.
A hidden world beneath the swell,
With each gentle wave, a secret to tell.

In the cooling breeze, ancient lore sings,
A chorus of time, to which the sea clings.
Embrace the mystery, let it unfold,
In depths of azure, let dreams be bold.

Charmed Stillness of the Ocean's Embrace

A gentle hush, a lover's sigh,
The ocean's arms, where hearts drift by.
Soft sands cradle weary souls,
In this stillness, the world feels whole.

Stars above, a twinkling guide,
In the ocean's bosom, our fears hide.
Kissed by calm, the spirit takes flight,
Woven dreams in the fabric of night.

Harmony whispers in every wave,
For those who listen, their hearts are brave.
In this embrace, find solace and grace,
The ocean's magic, a warm embrace.

Shadows of a Nautical Reverie

In twilight's grip, the waves do sigh,
A whispering breeze, the seagulls fly.
Moonlight dances on the deep blue sea,
Echoes of dreams, where we long to be.

Stars twinkle softly, like glimmers of hope,
Beneath the surface, where shadows elope.
Ghostly ships roam in the depths below,
Guided by tales only sailors know.

Rippling secrets in currents concealed,
Joys of the ocean, forever revealed.
In the heart of the storm, calm resides too,
For sailors who sail, and choose to renew.

With echoes of laughter, the night lingers on,
As visions of voyages gently are drawn.
Each splash of the water, a poet's refrain,
The sea holds our sorrows, and kisses our pain.

In shadows of dreams, we drift far away,
To realms of the heart where the mermaids play.
So raise your glass high, to the vast azure,
In shadows of nautical, we find our pure.

Dusk's Embrace in Marine Stillness

Beneath the horizon, where colors entwine,
Dusk weaves its magic, soft as fine wine.
Waves whisper secrets to the waiting shore,
In the cradle of twilight, we long for more.

Gentle the lullaby, nature's own song,
As tides ebb and flow, the night becomes strong.
In the heart of the stillness, the universe glows,
With mysteries hidden where the salty breeze blows.

Mirrors of starlight in waters so clear,
A tapestry woven with dreams we hold dear.
With each brush of twilight, our spirits unite,
In dusk's warm embrace, we find peace in the night.

Tender reflections, the moon's silver prize,
Kissing the ocean, under starlit skies.
With each fleeting moment, our souls reconnect,
In the dance of the waves, there's nothing to regret.

The sea's gentle rhythm, a heartbeat so true,
Guiding our dreams as the night bids adieu.
In the arms of the ocean, we find our way home,
Dusk's embrace whispers, we're never alone.

Harmonies Above the Sea Floor

Beneath the surface, where wonders reside,
The sea floor is singing, a treasure-filled tide.
Colorful creatures in a ballet of grace,
In this watery world, we find our place.

Corals like castles, where tides softly sway,
Each swish of the fins, like music at play.
Echoes of laughter in bubbles arise,
As dolphins weave tales under brightening skies.

Melodies carried by gentle sea streams,
Enchanting our eyes with the dance of our dreams.
Crabs chipperly scuttle, in a whimsical race,
In harmonies sung, we find our embrace.

Glimmers of sunlight paint patterns anew,
As sea turtles gracefully glide in the blue.
An orchestra thriving in waters so deep,
Where every note whispers secrets to keep.

In this world submerged, we set our hearts free,
With each rippling wave, we embrace the sea.
Harmonies flourish, forever they soar,
In the depths of the ocean, there's always more.

Nestling in Liquid Peace

Cradled in waters, I find my retreat,
Where currents enfold me in rhythmic heartbeat.
Nestling with dreams, a haven so wide,
In depths of the ocean, where secrets abide.

Gentle the embrace of each lapping wave,
A sanctuary found in the restless brine's cave.
Whispers of comfort in ripples that flow,
In this tranquil ballet, my spirit can grow.

Glimpses of wonder, like pearls in the gloom,
Color the silence, and fashion a bloom.
In the heart of the sea, I'm tenderly held,
Where worries dissolve, and magic is spelled.

The ebb and the flow, a soothing refrain,
A lullaby sung in the soft, salty rain.
With each gentle stroke, I drift ever near,
In liquid peace found, I shed every fear.

Floating in bliss, where time has no claim,
I nestle with dreams, for they feel the same.
In the heart of the ocean, love is the key,
I nestle forever, serene and free.

Ripples of a Dreamy Tide

In twilight's soft embrace, we drift,
Where shadows dance and stories sift.
The moon spills secrets on the sea,
Each wave a whisper, wild and free.

Beneath the stars, our dreams take flight,
As currents weave through the gentle night.
A lullaby of waves in bloom,
Awakens echoes in the gloom.

With every splash, our wishes soar,
In endless rhythm, hearts explore.
The tide knows paths we cannot see,
In every ripple, possibility.

From shore to shore, a magic thread,
We follow where the whispers led.
The ocean's breath, a calming breeze,
In this vast realm, our spirits tease.

So let us wander, hand in hand,
Through silver light on shifting sand.
For in the tide's enchanting sway,
Our dreams will dance, and never stray.

Tranquil Enchantment of the Deep

In depths of blue where silence reigns,
The heart finds peace, the spirit gains.
With every pulse of ocean's flow,
The mysteries of life we know.

Beneath the waves, where shadows play,
The world unfolds in shades of gray.
A soft enchantment, drifting near,
A melody that all can hear.

Coral castles, brightly glow,
In hues of emerald, deep and slow.
A gentle hush brings restless minds,
To rhythms that the sea unwinds.

As currents weave through threads of time,
We lose ourselves in whispers' rhyme.
The deep embraces, safe and wise,
A tranquil realm where magic lies.

So let us plunge into this space,
And find in stillness, warm embrace.
The enchanting depths, our souls shall keep,
In tranquil wonder, lost in sleep.

Pearls of Silence Around Us

In quietude, the ocean sighs,
Its secrets held beneath the skies.
Each pearl of silence, softly gleams,
Reflecting softly, quiet dreams.

The gentle tide, a soothing balm,
In rolling waves, the heart feels calm.
With every ebb, the world retreats,
In stillness found, the soul completes.

Beneath the stars, the waters hum,
A harmony that softly strums.
Each breath a note, a song of praise,
To nature's grace, in endless maze.

Amidst the calm, our worries cease,
In whispered winds, we find our peace.
The ocean's voice, a soft embrace,
A sanctuary of gentle grace.

So linger here, where silence dwells,
In tranquil tides, the heart compels.
With pearls of wisdom all around,
In quietude, true joy is found.

The Lull in Tidal Currents

When twilight falls, the world draws close,
The sea exhales, a gentle dose.
With every wave, a breath of night,
A lull that cradles, soft and light.

Phosphorescent glimmers weave their tale,
As tides recede, the night sets sail.
In whispered currents, dreams entwine,
A fluid dance, a secret sign.

The moon casts paths on waters wide,
Where wishes float, and hopes abide.
In every crest, the stars align,
A pointing finger, pure divine.

The lull invites our hearts to pause,
To marvel deeply, without flaws.
In tranquil moments, lost we find,
Sweet solace in the ocean's mind.

So let us cherish this serene space,
Where time suspends and leaves no trace.
In lullabies of tides that flow,
The heart discovers all it knows.

Whispers Beneath the Waves

Beneath the surf, the secrets lie,
Soft murmurs of the sea breeze sigh.
A tale of lost ships in moonlit gloom,
Where shadows dance in ocean's womb.

Each ripple tells of love and pain,
Of sailors who dared to dream and strain.
Their voices echo in watery halls,
As night wraps round with silken shawls.

The stars above, like diamonds bright,
Guide wandering hearts through velvet night.
With every wave that crashes down,
The sea breathes life, in silver crown.

From depths unknown, a soft refrain,
Calls out to those who dare to gain.
Awash in dreams, on currents wide,
The whispers beckon from the tide.

As dawn breaks forth, the silence bows,
To softest light, where stillness vows.
The ocean's heart shall never cease,
To sing its song, a tale of peace.

Silence of Waters Deep

In the stillness where spirits dwell,
The waters murmur secrets well.
Veils of mist rise, soft and bright,
Wrapping the world in calm delight.

Echoes of dreams in twilight's haze,
Shimmer like stars in ocean's gaze.
Time stands still in this quiet place,
Where whispers and shadows softly trace.

Beneath the waves, the past resides,
In the hush where mystery bides.
Each drop of salt, a story told,
In depths where ancient ghosts unfold.

From the polished rock to sandy shore,
The silence speaks of tales galore.
Secrets wrapped in twilight's fold,
Cradling memories, precious and bold.

In the heart of night, tranquility shines,
A chorus of thoughts in patterned lines.
The waters deep, a timeless keep,
Guarding the dreams that softly seep.

Echoes of Stillness by the Shore

The shore is kissed by gentle waves,
Where silence sings and courage braves.
Footprints linger, fading slow,
In the fading light, where the cool winds blow.

Each grain of sand a whispered plea,
A testament of what must be.
In the heart of dusk, shadows ascend,
Nature's quiet song, a faithful friend.

The horizon melts in colors warm,
Embracing night with a calming charm.
Ripples dance in the evening air,
Echoing dreams with tender care.

Oceans deep, where stillness reigns,
Cradling the world in soft refrains.
With every tide, a soft embrace,
Forgotten hopes find their resting place.

So let the magic linger near,
The whispers sweet, the joy sincere.
For in the stillness by the shore,
The echoes of life and love explore.

Lullabies from the Tide

A lullaby hums from ocean's crest,
Cradling dreams in their gentle nest.
The night sea sighs, a tender tune,
Beneath the glow of a silver moon.

Softening hearts, it sweeps along,
In hush of night where spirits throng.
Waves weave tales that time forgot,
In rhythms deep, by starlight caught.

The tide rolls in with soothing grace,
A timeless waltz, a warm embrace.
Each droplet sings of love and strife,
The ocean's pulse, the breath of life.

As shells rest close, with secrets bare,
A lullaby cradles the evening air.
In harmony with the moonlit skies,
The tides unveil their sweet goodbyes.

So close your eyes, let worries fade,
Listen to the songs the sea has made.
For in each wave, a tender light,
Lies lullabies from the deep of night.

Mists of Enchantment on Silent Shores

In twilight's glow where whispers play,
The mists of magic softly sway.
Ghostly forms in ebon light,
Dance along the shores of night.

Secrets held in sea-shells' coo,
Stories old yet always new.
Footsteps light on hidden sands,
Carved by fate's unseen hands.

Waves lap gently, tales unfold,
Of daring dreams and legends told.
The moon ascends with silver thread,
Awakening the things unsaid.

With each breath, the magic stirs,
Beneath the stars, the heart concurs.
On silent shores, the world stands still,
Wrapped in wonder, time will spill.

In morning's grace, the mists will part,
Leaving traces on a hopeful heart.
The magic lingers, soft and pure,
A timeless bond we all endure.

Harmonies of a Calm Cove

In a cove where laughter flows,
The gentle breeze of evening knows.
Tides in rhythm, softly sway,
Nature's song, a sweet ballet.

Seafoam whispers, secrets shared,
With every sigh, a heart is bared.
Pebbles glisten, kissed by light,
Echoes dance in fading night.

Harmony in colors blend,
Where ocean dreams and skies transcend.
A lullaby, the waves compose,
In tranquil depths, our spirit grows.

Stars above begin to weave,
Tales of worlds we dare believe.
Each note a magic thread we spin,
In this calm, our hearts begin.

As dawn awakens, softly bright,
The cove transforms with morning light.
Yet still, the echoes will remain,
In our souls, a sweet refrain.

The Lull of Enchanted Waters

Beneath the surface, secrets lie,
An ancient song, a silken sigh.
Ripples shimmer, dreams take flight,
In the hush of velvet night.

Moonlit paths on waters glide,
Where whispers of the deep abide.
Mirrored skies with stars aglow,
Guide the heart where waters flow.

Gentle waves caress the shore,
Cradling hopes forevermore.
In the lull, a spirit heals,
With every tide, the magic feels.

Stories whispered by the streams,
Craft the tapestry of dreams.
In liquid depths, our souls will dance,
Awakened by a fleeting glance.

As dawn approaches, all will fade,
Yet in the depths, the love we've laid.
The lull persists, a sweet embrace,
Enchanted waters, timeless space.

Ebbing Dreams on a Forgotten Beach

On sands where time has lost its way,
Ebbing dreams in twilight's sway.
Forgotten tales in shadows loom,
As dusk bequeaths the night its bloom.

Seashells murmur, soft and low,
Echoes of a long-lost flow.
Each grain of sand, a memory,
Carved by waves' soft symphony.

In salty air, the visions breathe,
Of laughter shared, and hearts to weave.
The shoreline stretches, timeless, vast,
Holding close the present, past.

With every tide, the dreams arise,
A dance of light beneath the skies.
Ebbing gently, they align,
In the beauty of the divine.

When dawn breaks forth with colors bright,
The beach awakens, kissed by light.
Yet in the hush of twilight's reach,
Linger still, this forgotten beach.

Serenity in the Depths of Indigo

In the embrace of twilight's hue,
Whispers dance on waters blue.
A lullaby from depths below,
Calming hearts with gentle flow.

Beneath the ripples, secrets lie,
Kissed by moonlight from the sky.
Each wave a tale of calm and grace,
In indigo's warm, enfolding space.

Stars ignite in mirrored seas,
Softly swaying with the breeze.
Reflecting dreams, they twinkling weave,
A tapestry that loves to believe.

Here, in silence, time stands still,
Echoing a quiet thrill.
Beneath the waves, the world unfurls,
Awash in magic, soft whirls.

With every breath, a moment's pause,
Nature's muse, life's gentle cause.
In the depths, where wonders roam,
A sanctuary we can call home.

The Breath of Shells and Secrets

Along the shore where dreams entwine,
Tales are written in the brine.
Shells by fortune's hands are cast,
Guarding whispers of the past.

The ocean's breath, a sigh of lore,
Unfolds its mysteries at the shore.
With every wave, a story brews,
Dancing shadows, timeless views.

Crabs and gulls in playful chase,
Spinning light among the lace.
Footprints left in glistening sand,
Signals of dreams, both wild and grand.

In twilight's grip, the silence swells,
Echoing the breath of shells.
As moonlight spills, secrets sing,
Nature's pulse, a vibrant ring.

Every grain a world concealed,
Life's rich tapestry revealed.
With every tide, potentials soar,
Shells of secrets, forevermore.

Tranquil Reflections on a Sea of Stars

As night descends, the heavens gleam,
In tranquil beauty, we dare to dream.
The ocean mirrors a cosmic dance,
Each wave a spark, a fleeting chance.

Crickets serenade the night's embrace,
While starlight winks with gentle grace.
In this reflection, hearts align,
Lost in the magic, endlessly fine.

The air is thick with whispered sighs,
As constellations weave the skies.
Ripples carry wishes near,
In the quiet calm, they disappear.

Beneath the stars, the sea does hum,
A melody of times to come.
In every shimmer, hope resides,
A tranquil heart where love abides.

And when the dawn begins to glow,
We'll hold the stars in memories slow.
For in this peace, we'll find our way,
Guided by night, to greet the day.

Hidden Melodies of the Watery Realm

In shadows deep, where silence reigns,
Melodies linger, soft refrains.
Whispers of fishes, songs of the deep,
A treasure trove where secrets creep.

Bubbles rise like laughter's kiss,
Echoing in the aquatic abyss.
Here, in this world of fluid grace,
Nature's choir finds its place.

Coral castles rock and sway,
Home to secrets of the bay.
Each note a ripple, clear and bright,
Filling the depths with pure delight.

With every tide, a tune reborn,
Lost in currents, a world adorned.
A symphony of life unfolds,
In watery realms, where stories are told.

So listen close to the silent song,
Of depths where we are meant to belong.
In hidden pools, let your spirit roam,
For in the water, we find our home.

The Pause Between the Swells

Before the wave, a hush resides,
A breath of sea, where time abides.
The ocean holds its secret close,
In quietude, the heart can pose.

A gull, it glides with perfect grace,
Its wings a brush, the sky a space.
The foamy edge, it whispers low,
With tales of depths where silence grows.

The ripples play, in soft ballet,
While sunlight dances on the spray.
Each moment stretches, time must hold,
While stories in the sea unfold.

The ship's old creak, the sailor's sigh,
As something stirs beneath the sky.
A fleeting glance, a fleeting thought,
In nature's pause, all dreams are caught.

Then sudden crash, the world awakes,
As watery mounts, the stillness breaks.
The swells reach forth, with power bold,
In rhythmic echoes, tales retold.

A Whispered Tale of Glistening Fins

In waters deep, where shadows sweep,
The fish do dance and secrets keep.
Their scales like jewels, bright and rare,
In fleeting moments, dreams declare.

Among the coral, soft and sweet,
A shimmer sings, beneath their feet.
Each flick of tail, a gentle plea,
A story told, beneath the sea.

With every rise and every fall,
They weave a song, a siren's call.
A whisper shared through currents wide,
In glistening fins, where magic hides.

The ocean's breath, a lullaby,
They glide through blue, beneath the sky.
In harmony, their voices blend,
A whispered tale that knows no end.

So dive into the liquid light,
Where fins like laughter take to flight.
Embrace the tale the waters spun,
In whispered dreams, we are as one.

Shadows Dancing in Calm Currents

In tranquil depths, where shadows play,
The waters hold the dance of day.
Beneath the wave, a tapestry,
Of light and dark, a mystery.

The gentle flow, a soft embrace,
As currents weave through timeless space.
Each shadow casts a fleeting gleam,
A world alive, within our dream.

In silver streaks, the fish do glide,
Through hidden paths, they softly bide.
With every pulse, the ocean sways,
In rhythmic tunes, it softly plays.

The whispers of the depths below,
In fluid grace, the secrets flow.
While shadows dance, both shy and bold,
In calm currents, their tale unfolds.

The world above, a distant hum,
While down below, the shadows come.
With every breath of ocean's air,
In shadows dancing, none may care.

The Silent Song of Sunken Shores

Where sunken shores meet silent seas,
The whispers of the past take ease.
With every grain of timeless sand,
A solemn tale of distant land.

The anchors rest, the wrecks decay,
In ocean's heart, they softly lay.
The seaweed sways, a gentle guide,
To legends deep where memories bide.

A distant ship, once proud and strong,
In echo's voice, it sings its song.
With currents gentle, tides unwind,
The silent song of those behind.

In twilight's glow, all secrets shine,
As hours trace the ocean's line.
Beneath the waves, in tranquil grace,
The sunken shores, a hidden place.

In watery realms, where silence drapes,
A world alive, a mystery shapes.
Through ocean's pulse, we find the score,
The silent song of sunken shores.

Shadows of Coral Dreams

In the depths where secrets sleep,
Coral whispers softly weep.
Shadows dance in twilight's glow,
Ancient tales of ebb and flow.

Glimmers fade with ocean's sigh,
Unseen wonders drift and fly.
In their hearts, the mysteries keep,
Guarding dreams that delve so deep.

A tide of colors, bright and bold,
Fables wrapped in blue and gold.
Each reef a story, each wave a rhyme,
Whirling whispers of forgotten time.

Beneath the brine, the mermaids hum,
To rhythmic drifts the sea does come.
Echoes blend in water's loom,
In shadows cast, old colors bloom.

So dive with grace, embrace the night,
Where coral dreams weave pure delight.
A world alight with mystic gleam,
Awaits within the shadows' seam.

The Hush of Distant Currents

Far beyond, where sea waves sway,
Distant currents find their play.
In silence soft, they weave a song,
Where oceans dream and spirits long.

Gentle tides, like time, they flow,
Echoing tales of long ago.
In whispered tones, they tell their lore,
Of lands unseen, of ocean's floor.

Seagulls glide in the quiet air,
Wings unfurl with graceful flair.
They ride the currents, fierce yet mild,
Nature's symphony, free and wild.

Deep below, the shadows stir,
In realms where vibrant colors blur.
The hush enfolds all earthly sound,
In braids of tides where dreams are found.

As night descends, the stars ignite,
Reflections dance in silvery light.
In hushed repose, the oceans breathe,
Their tales entwined, we dare believe.

Tranquil Reflections on Sand

Golden grains of softest touch,
Where footprints linger oh so much.
Waves retreat, in laughter blend,
Each moment's beauty, we suspend.

The sun dips low, a painted sky,
Whispers of dusk and day goodbye.
Clouds drift gently, pastel dreams,
In twilight's grace, the ocean gleams.

Seashell secrets, treasures found,
In every curve, a story bound.
The breeze of peace, a lover's sigh,
Inviting hearts to drift and fly.

With every step, the world feels right,
As stars emerge in deepening night.
Reflections cast on wet terrain,
A quiet moment held in vain.

Beneath the wide and endless dome,
The sand embraces, calls you home.
In tranquil echoes, spirits soar,
To dance again upon the shore.

Murmurs of the Sunken Realm

In the silent depths, shadows play,
Ancient whispers guide the way.
Forgotten dreams in water's weave,
In echoes soft, we dare believe.

Tides reveal what time has veiled,
The heart of ocean, untouched, hailed.
In currents swayed by moon's soft hand,
Murmurs arise from the sunken land.

Lost cities rest beneath the waves,
Guardians of the stories braves.
A treasure trove of tales untold,
In every fragment, history holds.

Fishes dance in colors bright,
In harmony, they weave through light.
Beneath the surface, life unfolds,
In muted tones, its beauty molds.

So listen close to the ocean's heart,
In every wave, a work of art.
The sunken realm, where magic gleams,
Awaits the seeker of ocean's dreams.

Hidden Depths of Hushed Bliss

In the quiet glen, the secrets dwell,
Whispers of the heart weave a gentle spell.
Sunlight dapples through the ancient trees,
Where laughter dances on the evening breeze.

Beneath the boughs, where dreams take flight,
Flickers of magic awaken the night.
Softly they shimmer, like stars above,
Each moment wrapped in the arms of love.

In the shade, where shadows play,
Time lingers softly, drifting away.
Like fleeting hopes on a passing sigh,
The depth of this peace makes the soul fly.

Amidst the blooms, a secret sings,
A lullaby carried on delicate wings.
Each petal, a promise, tender and near,
Whispers of joy that only we hear.

Where Dreams and Shadows Float

In twilight's embrace, the world turns gray,
Where dreams and shadows waltz and sway.
Each sigh of the night holds a thousand tales,
Of magic and wonder, where spirit prevails.

Beneath the moon, where the old trees stand,
Faint echoes whisper from the land.
Each flickering light offers a way,
To wander in realms where the heart may play.

Gentle starlight weaves through the air,
Dreams come alive with a touch of care.
They beckon the brave to dance with delight,
In the tender hush of the velvet night.

There's solace found in the shadows cast,
A journey through time, an adventure vast.
With each step forward, the heart learns to soar,
In a moment of wonder, forevermore.

The Still Waters of Mermaid Shadows

In the calm of the bay, where the moonlight glows,
Mermaid shadows linger, as the soft tide flows.
They sing to the depths, where the mysteries thrive,
In the stillness of night, the waters come alive.

Glimmers of laughter ripple through the sea,
As dreams intertwine with the heart's wild spree.
Cascades of silver like whispers they weave,
Promises hidden in what we believe.

Among the rocks, where the soft waves sigh,
Fables of enchantment float gently by.
Each droplet a memory of love's gentle touch,
In the silence we hold, it means ever so much.

With every wave, a new tale unfolds,
Of treasures and wonders more precious than gold.
The still waters glisten, reflecting our hearts,
Where the magic of mermaids constantly imparts.

Chimes of Tranquility in the Tide

As day meets the dusk, the chimes softly ring,
A lullaby carried by the whispering spring.
The ocean's embrace sings a sweet refrain,
Of memories cherished, and joy without pain.

In the hush of the evening, serenity blooms,
Accompanied gently by the sea's soft tunes.
Each wave brings a promise, a gentle caress,
Wrapped in the stillness, our hearts find their rest.

The quiver of sand underfoot, so divine,
As time melds with tides, all worries decline.
Here, the heart wanders, unshackled and free,
In the echoes of nature, we're meant to be.

With every moonrise, the magic ignites,
Painting the heavens with shimmering lights.
The chimes of tranquility whisper of peace,
In the dance of the tides, our troubles release.

Lurking Whispers of the Sea

In the depths where shadows creep,
Whispers linger, secrets sleep.
Beneath the waves, a world concealed,
Mysteries of the ocean revealed.

Moonlit tides in silence sway,
Guiding souls who drift away.
With salt and song, the currents blend,
Stories of the deep, they send.

Echoes of a time untold,
Characters in myths grow bold.
Creatures dance in fluid grace,
Haunting dreams that time can trace.

Bubbles rise from sandy beds,
Carrying whispers of the dead.
The sea, a keeper of the lore,
Calls to hearts longing for more.

In twilight's glow, where legends blend,
The ocean speaks, a timeless friend.
Each wave that crashes, a soft caress,
Guiding lost souls to happiness.

Underwater Poise of Nature

Amidst the shifts of azure blue,
Life's ballet, so pure, so true.
Gentle sways of coral reefs,
In harmony, the ocean breathes.

Fins like brushes, strokes of art,
Each creature plays a vital part.
Beneath the surface, a world so vast,
In underwater realms, dreams are cast.

Emerald plants sway with ease,
Swaying softly in the breeze.
Their colors burst, a painter's scheme,
Nature's canvas, painted dream.

Tiny fish in silver schools,
Dance to rhythms, wordless rules.
A symphony of sounds and sights,
In the depths where magic ignites.

Serpentine shapes glide through the gloom,
Graceful shadows in the bloom.
In this wonder, life unfolds,
A story that the ocean holds.

Resting Waves and Dreaming Tails

Waves that curl in soft embrace,
Whispers of a tranquil place.
Tails that flicker, dreams that soar,
In the depths, they seek for more.

Beneath the surface, silence reigns,
Echoes dance, unchained by chains.
In slumber's grasp, the ocean sighs,
As the moonbeams touch the skies.

Dressed in hues of twilight skies,
Fluttering fins with watchful eyes.
A world where every ripple speaks,
Of the treasures that the ocean seeks.

For every wave that crashes down,
A story waits, a hidden crown.
The tides will tell of joys and fears,
In salty tears through endless years.

As night descends, the sea finds peace,
In slumber's hold, all cares release.
Here, the dreams are wild and free,
Nestled deep beneath the sea.

Slumbering Echoes on Siren Shores

On the shore where sirens call,
Echoes linger, rise, and fall.
Softly sing the tales unknown,
In their lilt, the past is sown.

Seashell whispers in the night,
Carried gently, pure delight.
With every cresting wave, a tune,
Melodies beneath the moon.

Dreamers find their hearts align,
In the dance of sea and brine.
As stars blink in the velvet skies,
The ocean reflects our sighs.

Sand beneath, a warm caress,
Holding secrets to confess.
A tapestry of dreams entwined,
In the gentle tide, we're aligned.

So rest your head and drift away,
Let the siren's song display.
For in these echoes, life's embrace,
We find our true and sacred place.

Secrets Lain Still in the Abyss

In the depths where shadows creep,
Whispers of old secrets sleep.
Forgotten tales, in silence dwell,
Guardians of a mystic spell.

Echoes of dreams from ages past,
They weave their spells, shadows cast.
Tales of woe and glimmers bright,
In the abyss, they hide from light.

Beneath the waves, time stands still,
Haunted by a potent thrill.
Visions shrouded in dark embrace,
Lost in the depths, a hidden place.

From ancient depths, spirits call,
In an ocean, vast and enthralled.
Secrets buried, longing to rise,
Yet in silence, they wear their disguise.

Glimmers of hope in shadows roam,
The abyss, a home, a lost dome.
In the stillness, they softly sigh,
Echoing as forgotten dreams fly.

Embrace of Soft Undercurrents

Gentle tides caress the shore,
Whispers of currents, a secret lore.
In the embrace of the ocean's sway,
Soft undulations guide the way.

Moonlight dances on silken waves,
Painting dreams in water's caves.
Underneath, a world unknown,
Cradles the hearts that have grown.

In twilight's glow, the waters hum,
Voices calling, we become.
The undercurrents pull us deep,
In their thrall, awaken to sleep.

Ripples carry tales anew,
Of lives lived, of love, too.
Embracing all, fierce and tender,
Secrets shared — we softly surrender.

The ocean's pulse, a guiding hand,
Leads us to a forgotten land.
With each breath, the currents flow,
In their dance, we learn to grow.

Serene Echoes of the Sea's Heartbeat

In the still of dawn, whispers speak,
The sea's heartbeat, calm yet meek.
Serenity wrapped in a gentle sigh,
A lullaby sung beneath the sky.

Waves embrace the sandy shore,
Tales of journeys forevermore.
Beneath the surface, a rhythmic song,
A promise that we all belong.

Every pulse tells of a time,
Of mariners, myths, and chimes.
In echoes soft, the past awakes,
As the ocean's heart steadily breaks.

Glistening tides on a quiet morn,
Turn dreams to life, not to be torn.
Listening close, we hear the call,
In the sea's heart, love envelops all.

Serene moments in salty air,
Unfurl the peace beyond compare.
With every wave, our worries fade,
In the ocean's arms, we're remade.

A Serenade for Lost Souls Below

Beneath the waves where spirits dwell,
A serenade, a haunting bell.
Echoing soft through depths unseen,
For those who wander in between.

Melodies swirl in the ocean's breath,
Singing of life, of love, of death.
Lost souls drifting, hearts entwined,
In the sea's grip, solace they find.

Carried forth on currents wide,
In their dance, no need to hide.
Each note a tale, a timeless thread,
Weaving stories for the dead.

Waves roll on, whisper their name,
In this chorus, none are the same.
Together they sing, a lilting tune,
Under the light of a silver moon.

For in this realm where shadows play,
Lost souls find peace in the ocean's sway.
In symphony with the sea's embrace,
They carry on through time and space.

The Enchantment of the Glistening Surface

Upon the lake, a shimmer bright,
Reflects the stars in the soothing night.
Ripples dance with soft delight,
A spellbound hush, all feels just right.

Moonlight drapes on water's skin,
A beckoning call, where dreams begin.
Secrets swirl and softly spin,
As magic glows from deep within.

Each drop of dew, a tale untold,
In whispers soft, the stories unfold.
The surface glimmers, brave and bold,
A charm that never gets too old.

Glistening waves, a fleeting kiss,
In nature's arms, a perfect bliss.
Here I linger, caught in this,
The enchantment sings, I can't dismiss.

Wonders wait on the glistening crest,
Each moment savored, each heartbeat pressed.
Magic flows, we feel so blessed,
In the lake's embrace, we find our rest.

Whispers on the Windward Waters

The breeze it sighs, a gentle song,
Upon the waves where hearts belong.
With every breath, the night feels strong,
A lullaby where dreams prolong.

Chasing clouds in the twilight's glow,
A dance of feathers, soft and slow.
Nature's chorus, a soothing flow,
In every whisper, love we'll sow.

The water sparkles, secrets thrive,
In moonlit paths where spirits dive.
Whispers beckon, alive, alive,
As night unveils, our souls revive.

Through rustling leaves and silver tides,
Adventures wait where peace abides.
In gentle breath, the heart confides,
In whispered tones, the soul resides.

With every gust, the world unwinds,
The dance of the wind, serenity finds.
Together here, our spirit binds,
Upon these waters, love reminds.

The Gossamer Touch of a Gentle Sea Breeze

A feathered breeze drifts softly near,
With whispers of salt, the ocean's cheer.
It wraps around, a tender sphere,
In nature's hug, we hold it dear.

The shoreline sings a calming tune,
Beneath the watchful, silver moon.
Whispers rise as stars commune,
In the stillness, dreams are strewn.

Waves brush gently, a lover's hand,
Caressing shores of golden sand.
Each grain a story, perfectly planned,
In the breeze's dance, we understand.

Morning light spills across the sea,
Awakening hearts, wild and free.
In gossamer touch, we come to be,
Bonded in magic, just you and me.

As day unfolds, the journey calls,
With every rise, the spirit enthralls.
In the gentle breeze, peace gently falls,
Together we weave, where love enthralls.

Rapture of Peace in Deep Waters

In quiet depths, serenity lies,
Where ripples hush and silence sighs.
Mysterious worlds beneath the skies,
In deep waters, my spirit flies.

A canvas painted with shades of blue,
Moments linger, pure and true.
The dance of life, a gentle view,
In the depths, my heart anew.

Sweet silence drapes like velvet night,
Under the waves, there's pure delight.
In echoes soft, the stars ignite,
With every breath, we feel the light.

Here in the calm, the soul finds grace,
A sanctuary, a sacred space.
Time stands still, we leave no trace,
In deep waters, we embrace.

Rapture waits in the stillness deep,
Where dreams awaken from slumber's sweep.
In the heart of the sea, love we keep,
In peace we linger, forever steep.

Mellow Melodies of Submerged Shores

Gentle waves caress the sand,
Where whispers of the sea expand.
The tides in dance, a soft ballet,
With secrets in the deep, they sway.

Beneath the moon's tender embrace,
Shells shimmer bright, a hidden grace.
Each note a lullaby so sweet,
Where ocean dreams and silence meet.

In twilight hues, the waters gleam,
A world awash in twilight's dream.
The shoals reflect a starry sigh,
As lullabies of currents lie.

Soft lullabies weave through the night,
Cradled in the ocean's light.
Each soft ripple sings its tune,
A melody to the silver moon.

On shores where time knows no despair,
And every breeze becomes a prayer.
These mellow sounds, they drift away,
In rhythm with the break of day.

Ephemeral Silence on Briny Breaths

In the stillness where seas repose,
Soft whispers ride on evening's close.
Briny breaths that come and go,
In twilight's glow, emotions flow.

The hush of tides, a fleeting sound,
In quiet depths, lost treasures found.
Each wave a memory, soft, unclear,
Ephemeral whispers, crystal clear.

Stars blink from the heavens above,
A serenade of ocean love.
Time drifts on, a slow ballet,
In silence, dreams will gently sway.

Salted air, a tender kiss,
In the night's arms, a moment's bliss.
The ocean's heart, a pulsing sigh,
Where dreams are born and hopes can fly.

A lull of peace upon the shore,
Each breath a promise, here we pour.
In waves, we find a resting place,
Where silence binds the ocean's grace.

The Stillness of Forgotten Depths

In depths where sunlight cannot find,
Lies a world of shadows well-defined.
Forgotten tales in silence wait,
Adrift in currents, sealed by fate.

With every pulse, the ocean breathes,
In stillness woven into reeds.
Secrets whisper through the blue,
Lost echoes of a life once true.

Anemones dance in the gloom,
While time spins webs in darkling bloom.
Still waters cradle fragile dreams,
Where light fades low and silence beams.

In this realm, all thoughts dissolve,
As mysteries of the deep evolve.
A symphony of muted hues,
In forgotten depths, we glean our views.

Vast and deep, the ocean sighs,
A lonely hymn beneath the skies.
Within the stillness, life remains,
In hushed embrace, where beauty reigns.

Tranquil Essence of the Ocean's Heart

Beneath the waves, a gentle pulse,
Where tranquil waters softly waltz.
The ocean's heart, a calming beat,
With every tide, a cycle sweet.

In azure depths, the silence calls,
A soothing calm where rippling falls.
In harmony with every flow,
The essence of the sea will show.

Coral gardens, vibrant hues,
In this realm, the soul renews.
Each breath we take, a song of peace,
In ocean's splendor, all worries cease.

The world above fades far away,
Embraced in dreams where spirits play.
The tranquil depths invite us near,
To find ourselves, to disappear.

So let us dive in soft embrace,
To seek the heart in this vast space.
In waves of calm, we'll gently part,
Consumed by the ocean's tranquil heart.

The Calm After the Swells

The waves have whispered all their tales,
Where foam meets shore, the heart exhales.
Beneath the sky, a tranquil hue,
The ocean sighs, the world anew.

The gulls now rest upon the sand,
Their cries subdued, the day is bland.
The sun dips low, a golden gleam,
In quietude, we dare to dream.

The tides retreat, a soft embrace,
While shadows stretch, they slow their chase.
In this hush, where moments freeze,
We find our peace among the trees.

With every breath, the air is light,
As stars emerge from cloaks of night.
The sea reflects the moon's soft glow,
In silence sweet, our spirits flow.

The calm descends, a soothing balm,
In twilight's grasp, we find our calm.
The world holds still, the heart's delight,
For in this space, all wrong feels right.

Where Shadows Dance in Stillness

In twilight's grip, the shadows sway,
They weave their tales at end of day.
Beneath the trees, where secrets keep,
The whispers linger, soft and deep.

The moonlight bathes the earth in grace,
While shadows twirl, an elegant pace.
Each rustling leaf, a gentle sigh,
In cool embrace where time drifts by.

A flicker here, a glimmer there,
As stars emerge from velvet air.
The night embraces with its cloak,
In quietude, the silence spoke.

Dancing lightly, the shadows play,
As dreams unfurl and drift away.
A moment held, both firm and light,
In stillness found, we find our night.

With every pulse, the world awaits,
The dawn to break, as fate relates.
Yet here we stand, in shadows' trance,
Where time suspends and hearts advance.

Songs of Serenity in Salty Air

The ocean sings a soothing tune,
Where seagulls glide beneath the moon.
In salty air, sweet breezes roam,
And waves compose a quiet home.

The sun ignites the water's face,
A dance of light, a warm embrace.
With every crash upon the shore,
The heart finds peace, forevermore.

Each splash a note, a song so clear,
Inviting all who choose to hear.
The horizon whispers distant calls,
Where dreams set sail and freedom sprawls.

The tides may change, but here we stand,
With footprints pressed in silver sand.
In moments held 'neath a lavender sky,
Our spirits soar, our worries fly.

In twilight's glow, the sea now sighs,
As stars awaken in darkened skies.
With songs of peace, we weave our prayer,
In harmony found, in salty air.

Beneath the Surface

Beneath the waves, a world concealed,
Where mysteries wait, and hearts are healed.
A dance of colors, vivid and bright,
In depths so tranquil, veiled from light.

Coral kingdoms stretch and sway,
In silent songs where dreams hold sway.
The whispers of fish, their tales untold,
In emerald gardens where life unfolds.

With every drop, a secret lies,
In shimmering pools, where magic thrives.
The gentle sway of seaweed's grace,
In this cool embrace, we find our place.

Time flows softly like the tide,
In caverns dark where wonders hide.
The heart learns stillness, deep and wide,
While nature's heartbeat sings inside.

So let us dive into the blue,
Where silence sings and skies are true.
For beneath the surface, life does bloom,
In joyous light, we cast off gloom.

All is Calm

In the heart of night, still waters lie,
As stars twinkle in the velvet sky.
The world slows down, the breath is light,
In this cocoon, all is right.

The whispers fade, the hum subsides,
As moonlight washes the ocean's tides.
Each gentle wave, a soothing balm,
In silent moments, we find our calm.

The trees stand tall, the shadows blend,
In tranquil solace, we transcend.
With every sigh, we spill our fears,
And in the quiet, wipe our tears.

The night embraces with tender care,
While dreams take flight on silver air.
With every heartbeat, time does flow,
In this stillness, we come to know.

So close your eyes and just be here,
Where peace envelops, soft and clear.
For in this grace, we rest our psalm,
In harmony sweet, all is calm.

Whispers Beneath the Tidal Veil

Beneath the waves, the secrets lie,
Whispers soft as the seagull's cry.
In shadows cast by moonlit dreams,
The ocean's heart softly gleams.

Tales of sailors lost in time,
Chasing stars with hopes that climb.
A lullaby of tides that weave,
Stories that the deep will cleave.

In coral caves where echoes play,
Mermaids dance, and dolphins sway.
Their voices blend with the ocean's sigh,
A serenade that will not die.

The rhythmic pulse, a tranquil beat,
Guiding souls on salty feet.
Here where the world begins to fade,
Magic lingers, unafraid.

So listen close, in twilight's glow,
To whispers soft from depths below.
For in the hush of night's embrace,
The tides reveal their mystic grace.

Echoes in the Siren's Wake

Through foam and spray, a songbird flies,
A siren's call beneath the skies.
Cascading notes, like silver beams,
Enchant the heart with woven dreams.

In hidden coves, where shadows dwell,
The depths conceal a haunting spell.
Lost to the world, they hum and sway,
Echoing in the twilight's gray.

With every wave that breaks and sighs,
The ocean weeps, the ocean cries.
Yet in the depths, a joy remains,
A symphony that never wanes.

Beneath the surface, calm and wide,
Their laughter dances with the tide.
In swirling eddies, secrets twirl,
As whispers kiss the ocean's pearl.

To foreign shores, the stories drift,
In gentle waves, the memories lift.
A siren's song, forever near,
In every heart, forever clear.

Silence Beneath the Ocean's Lullaby

In aquatic halls, where silence reigns,
A lullaby threads through hidden chains.
With every pulse, the water sings,
Of ancient worlds and timeless things.

A harmony within the blue,
Cradles dreams that feel so true.
Soft ripples echo through the night,
Guiding hearts with gentle light.

Here in the depths, the darkness blooms,
A garden rich with secret rooms.
Mystic shadows, softly drawn,
Whispering tales of dusk till dawn.

The currents weave a velvet thread,
Binding souls that love not dread.
In quiet depth, the world unfurls,
Embracing all with tender swirls.

So close your eyes to the tempest bright,
And drift away into the night.
For beneath the waves, peace will lie,
In silence soft as the ocean's sigh.

The Stillness Where Waves Whisper

Where land meets sea, a stillness falls,
And nature's breath, enchantment calls.
The gentle lapping, a soothing sound,
In this quiet, magic's found.

With every tide, a story sways,
Of sunlit shores and starlit ways.
The pebbles murmur, secrets shared,
In whispers soft, the world is spared.

The moonlight dances on liquid glass,
Where dreams and ocean's heart amass.
In tranquil calm, the spirits sigh,
For in this stillness, time slips by.

Within the depths, old legends stir,
Lived long ago, yet still recur.
In harmony with waves that play,
The past awakens with the day.

So linger here, in the twilight's glow,
Where mystery wanders, free to flow.
For in the stillness where waves meet,
Eternity rests, serene and sweet.

Stillness in the Ocean's Embrace

In the hush where the waves do sigh,
Beneath the sky of cerulean hue,
Secrets whisper in currents shy,
Embraced by depths, both old and new.

Stars twinkle like the dreams of night,
Glistening upon the tranquil sea,
As the moon lends her silver light,
The ocean cradles thoughts, so free.

Bubbles dance in a ballet rare,
While coral gardens weave their tale,
A symphony of peace to share,
Within the womb of waves, we sail.

Drifting deeper, hear the hum,
Nature's heartbeat, soft and slow,
In the silence, we come undone,
Found in the tides, we feel the flow.

As horizons blend, both near and far,
The sea's embrace, a soft caress,
In the stillness, we find our star,
And in her arms, we find our rest.

Ghostly Currents in Twilight

Beneath the cover of twilight's veil,
The ocean whispers secrets deep,
Veiled figures in a moonlit trail,
Ghostly currents where shadows creep.

Phantoms dance on the foam-tipped waves,
With stories woven into the night,
Echoes of sailors, lost and brave,
Lure us gently with their plight.

In the chill of the evening's breath,
Songs of yore begin to unfold,
Each whisper carries tales of death,
And treasures lost in depths untold.

Flickers of light in the water's sway,
Guide our hearts on a spectral quest,
In the twilight, the spirits play,
Seeking solace, they seek their rest.

Through the sea, we hear the call,
Of stories weaving through the night,
In ghostly currents, we find it all,
Life's woven tapestry, dark and bright.

The Calm Between Tides

In the quiet, just before the rise,
The world holds breath, in silence sleeps,
Hope blooms gentle in the skies,
A tranquil heart, the ocean keeps.

Soft whispers of the water's sighs,
Kissing the shore with tender grace,
Time suspends, as daylight flies,
In this moment, a sacred space.

Seagulls nestle, they find their peace,
While soft sands cradle dreams anew,
In calmness, worries start to cease,
As the ocean shares its hue.

Each ripple brings a tale of lore,
Of ebbing fears and longing tears,
In between tides, we seek for more,
Where distance fades and hope appears.

Lost in stillness, the heart is free,
To dance with dreams and wander wide,
In the calm, we glimpse what will be,
As the tides of life gently abide.

Secrets of the Abyss

In shadows deep where sunlight fades,
The ocean holds its treasures tight,
Secrets burrowed in dark cascades,
Waiting for the daring light.

Whispers echo through coral halls,
Ancient tales of love and lore,
In the depths where the darkness calls,
Legends wait on the ocean floor.

Creatures glide in a silent dance,
Wings unfurl beneath the waves,
In their eyes, there's a haunted trance,
Guardians of the lost, the brave.

With every dive, we search for truth,
Unravel threads of time's design,
In the abyss, we reclaim our youth,
And discover what is truly divine.

As we plunge into the twilight blue,
The mysteries of the deep unfold,
Each secret shared, a journey new,
In the ocean's heart, our stories told.

www.ingramcontent.com/pod-product-compliance
Ingram Content Group UK Ltd.
Pitfield, Milton Keynes, MK11 3LW, UK
UKHW050518050225
4438UKWH00043B/13